Unde
Shares
in a Day

Ian Bruce

TAKE THAT LTD.

Take That Ltd.
P.O.Box 200
Harrogate
HG1 2YR

You should take independent financial advice before acting on material contained in this book.

Printed and bound in Great Britain.

ISBN 1-873668-41-4

Contents

ACKNOWLEDGEMENTS

Thanks to my wife Pauline for her usual patience and assistance in making this work possible.

Finally, this book is dedicated to my daughter Hannah Lea, who has taught me that some of the best things in life just aren't quantifiable.

Ian Bruce, 1997

Also by the same author...

Understand Bonds & Gilts in a Day

... and in the same series...

Understand Derivatives in a Day
Understand Financial Risk in a Day

PREFACE

MOST PEOPLE refer to "stocks and shares" from time to time during the course of normal conversation, but few know exactly what types of shares are available to the investing public and even fewer understand how they work.

Understand Shares in a Day aims to put that right. This concise guide explains in simple terms exactly what shares are, how they work in relation to the stock market and how anyone can begin profiting from shares as safely as possible. *The aim is **not** specifically to encourage you to invest in shares, but to give you enough knowledge about the subject so that you can make an informed decision as to whether they would be useful in helping you to achieve your investment goals.*

As a starting point, you are given a working definition for what shares represent. Then you find out about the different types of shares that are currently available, and see how they can be bought and sold. This section of the book also includes a guide to selecting a broker who is most suited to your investment needs.

Following this, you will look at the role of investment and unit trusts - vehicles which can help any investor to spread the risks associated with shares whilst still leaving lots of room for potential profits. In the same vein, you will discover how it is possible to build a share portfolio to spread risk and help achieve your investment goals.

Even the more experienced financial investor will benefit from discussions about penny shares, share valuation, technical analysis and the use of equity options as tools which can provide at least some level of protection from falling share prices.

All in all, *Understand Shares in a Day* will help you decide if investing in shares is for you. Whatever your level of previous investing experience, you can be sure that the information contained in this handy title will contribute to your knowledge, and perhaps even to your bank account.

Introduction

JUST A FEW decades ago, share-ownership was something enjoyed by an elite and prosperous minority. To own shares in just one company - let alone a whole selection of companies - was something of a status symbol.

Not so in the 1990's. Today, share ownership is more popular than ever, and anyone who cares to do a little research can find several ways of making potentially profitable investments - whether they want to invest a fortune or just a few hundred pounds.

This rise in popularity has changed the face of private investment forever. Now many people are just as interested in finding out how their shares have fluctuated as they are in finding out what the latest weather forecast predicts. With many building societies converting to banks, millions of everyday people have received 'windfall shares' and are exploring the possibilities of the stock market as eagerly as NASA scientists explore the surface of Mars.

In short, share ownership has never been more popular.

Shares are bought and sold on the **stock-market**. This is much like any other market, but here the products on offer are stocks and commodities. Buying and selling is done through **brokers** who act as middle-men between prospective investors and the companies which have made their shares available to the public.

Why Do People Buy Shares?

There are many different types of shares available, and just as many reasons for buying them. Some people want to prepare financially for a future goal or event, such as retirement or the purchase of a home.

Others just want to make their savings work as hard as possible. Still others treat the stock market like a casino, buying and selling high-risk shares in the hope of making big profits as quickly as possible.

In a nutshell, the benefits of shares are:

✔   They can help an investor to make far more profit than he would if he left his money in a simple building society or bank deposit account.

✔   They can give the investor a great level of control over his personal finances.

✔   They can, over the long term, generate profits which vastly outperform normal interest rates.

Unfortunately, shares also have a major downside. Namely:

✘   Their values can go down as well as up, causing the investor to lose some or even all of his original investment.

The Key To Successful Investing

The key to successful investing in any financial product is to have a good level of knowledge. The more you know and understand about shares and how to select them, the more chance you will have of showing a good profit over the long term. The main areas of knowledge you will need to develop are:

Product knowledge

There are many different types of shares and not all are suitable for any particular investment goal. Knowing which type of share is most suited to your investment needs is essential.

Arithmetical knowledge

Having some knowledge of simple arithmetical calculations will enable you to evaluate a share before you actually decide whether or not to buy it. This will not only help you to save wasting time, but it will also help you confirm if the share in question is really worth buying in the first place.

Strategic knowledge

There are a number of different investment strategies which can help you to reduce the amount of risk you expose yourself to when dealing with shares. Understanding these strategies and using them wisely could mean the difference between suffering a devastating loss and making a good profit.

Chapter One

Shares

A Working Definition

> KEY FEATURE: A share is exactly what the name
> suggests - a share in the financial future of a company.

THE BASIC PRINCIPLE works like this: If a company is started by ten people who each invest £100, then the company is worth £1,000 and each **share-holder** owns one tenth of the whole. Should the company do well and make money, then each shareholder will receive a portion of the profits equal to their share-holding - in this case ten per cent each. This payout is called a **dividend**. Alternatively, the company directors may keep the profits in the company, in which case the value of the shares will rise.

Say the profits are £500 for the year. Each investor will receive £50 by way of a dividend. Or, if the profits are retained, the company will be worth £1,500 and each share will have increased in value from £100 to £150.

If the company doesn't do well and actually loses £700 then the company is now worth just £300 and the value of each share will have fallen from £100 to just £30. In addition, no dividend will be payable because no profits have been made.

Of course, this is just a theoretical example of how shares work. In reality, there may be millions of share-holders for any one company and some of them will hold more shares than others. Nevertheless, the principle remains the same and shareholders receive a share of the company's profits or losses in direct proportion to the number of shares they own.

Shares are issued by companies for two major reasons. The first is to fund some kind of expansion, such as the building of a new production plant, opening a new research laboratory or broadening their product range. Issuing shares in the company helps to raise the necessary capital to achieve these aims, and will hopefully result in the company reaching a greater level of profitability.

The second major reason for issuing shares is to avoid taking out loans. Loans, whether taken from a bank or from the public via fixed interest securities, require a certain amount of interest to be paid regardless of how well or poorly the company performs in the coming years. If the company does well, that's fine, but if it doesn't do as well as it hopes, the interest on loans is still payable. Shareholders, however, would receive dividends which directly reflect the amount of profit the company makes. This means that if the company doesn't do so well, the dividends paid to shareholders would naturally be lower than any interest payable on a comparable loan.

From the investors point of view, buying shares gives them a very real stake in the financial future of the company they invest in. If the company grows then their shares will increase in value and so will the dividends they receive each year. Of course, if the company fails then the value of their shares will fall - but that is the kind of risk a share investor is prepared to take in the hope of making potential profits.

Share Types

There are many kinds of shares available. The most common ones are:

> Ordinary Shares
> Preference Shares
> Cumulative Preference Shares
> Redeemable Preference Shares
> Convertible Preference Shares
> Deferred Shares
> Bearer Shares
> Penny Shares

Each of these share types have their own key features and appeal to different types of investors, so now we will discuss them individually in turn...

Ordinary Shares

Also referred to as equities, ordinary shares are the most common type of shares in the modern market. They give the share-holder the right to vote at share-holder meetings on the future of the company, normally on a vote-per-share basis. This means that for every share he holds, he has one vote. Ten shares equal ten votes, and so on.

All ordinary share-holders receive the same dividends in direct proportion to the size of their holdings. A person who owns 1,000 ordinary shares will therefore receive twice as much as someone who owns 500 shares, but only half as much as a person who owns 2,000.

If a company is forced into liquidation, owners of ordinary shares are placed at the bottom of the list as far as payments to creditors are concerned. So it is quite possible that the ordinary share-holder may not get back any of his initial investment. This is a worst case scenario, but it is important to realise that it can happen all the same.

Ordinary shares issued by the very biggest companies are often referred to as **blue chip** shares. These are thought of as being as safe as ordinary shares can get, simply because blue chip companies have a track record of outstanding success and are not likely to disappear overnight.

Preference Shares

As their name suggests, preference shares give the share-holders preference over ordinary share-holders in the list of payments to creditors. This means that if a company goes into liquidation, a holder of preference shares will be paid before ordinary share-holders and so there is more chance of him recouping at least some of his initial investment.

Often, the dividend payable on preference shares is fixed and is not likely to fluctuate from year to year. There are some exceptions to this, however, and so you should always check the specific details of any preference share before buying.

Cumulative Preference Shares

These are the same as preference shares, with one major difference. If dividends have been unpaid at any point, the share-holder may be able to claim these dividends at a later date. Dividends are therefore said to be cumulative.

Redeemable Preference Shares

These have fixed repayment dates, allowing the investor to plan his financial affairs with some precision as far as time is concerned. Redeemable preference shares are more like loans than true shares, but currently the financial markets make no formal distinction.

Convertible Preference Shares

Convertible Preference Shares are interesting because they can be converted to ordinary shares on specific dates at predetermined rates. This means that if the company which issued convertible preference shares does particularly well, the shareholder has the opportunity (but not the obligation) to convert to ordinary shares and enjoy a capital gain.

Deferred Shares

These are shares which do not normally qualify for dividends until a predetermined date or profit level has been achieved by the company which issues them. They do, however, normally give the shareholder some of the benefits associated with other types of shares, such as the right to vote at shareholder meetings and some comeback in the event of the company in question going into liquidation.

Bearer Shares

As their name suggests, bearer shares belong to the person who holds (or "bears") the share certificate. Dividend payments are not sent out automatically but must be claimed by the bearer - normally by mailing a claim coupon. Bearer shares are more commonly used in other European countries than they are in the United Kingdom, but investors who want to keep their activities particularly discreet use them quite regularly since no register of shareholders is kept.

Penny Shares

There is no clear-cut definition of "a Penny Share". A decade ago investors may have said that a penny share was any share costing less than 30p. Today some say that a penny share is any share costing less than 90p. This figure will undoubtedly be revised again in future years as shares in the broader market become more expensive. Penny shares are a subject in their own right and will be covered in much greater depth in Chapter Six.

Essential Terminology

Before closing this chapter and beginning a discussion on how the share market actually works, it is necessary to define some essential share-related terminology so that you fully understand what is being said later on in this book. Here then, is a crash-course in investment jargon...

Rights Issues

If a company has already issued shares but wishes to raise more capital, it may offer existing shareholders the opportunity to buy more. This is known as a rights issue.

Scrip Issues

If a company has already issued shares but wishes to increase the number of shares in circulation, it may give additional shares to existing shareholders on an "x for y" basis. This would be a scrip issue. For example, if a shareholder has ten £10 shares in a particular company, he may be given a scrip issue on a "five for one" basis. This might result in ten £10 shares being taken and replaced with fifty £2 shares. Note that because no additional capital has been injected into the company, the value of the new shares is proportionately decreased so that the shareholder neither gains or loses financially from the scrip issue.

New issues

When a company is floated on the stock exchange and offers shares for the very first time, these are said to be new issues.

Fixed Interest Stocks

Fixed interest stocks are normally referred to as either Bonds or Gilts. A bond is a promise from a company to pay a lender of money a fixed sum of interest on a regular basis for a stated period. In other words, the person who invests in a bond is not buying any equity in the company but is simply making a loan to the company in return for a fixed sum of interest and a promise of eventual repayment. A gilt is similar, but in this case the investor lends money to the government to help the building of new schools, roads and other projects which should improve the productivity of the country.

Investing in fixed interest stocks is a specialist subject in its own right. If you are interested in studying this subject further, please refer to another book in this series entitled *Understand Bonds & Gilts in a Day*.

Cum-Dividend

A stock or share which is described as being cum-dividend is one which is being offered with the dividend included. For example, if an investor buys a cum-dividend share one week before the dividend payment date, he will receive all monies which have accumulated since the last dividend payment date, even though this may have been six months ago.

Ex-Dividend

A stock or share which is described as being ex-dividend is one which is being offered with the dividend excepted. For example, if our investor buys an ex-dividend share four months before the next dividend payment date, he will not be entitled to receive a dividend on that occasion.

Summary

✔ A share is exactly what the name suggests - a share in the financial future of a company.

✔ There are many kinds of shares available. The most common are: Ordinary Shares, Preference Shares, Cumulative Preference Shares, Redeemable Preference Shares, Convertible Preference Shares, Deferred Shares, Bearer Shares and Penny Shares.

✔ Ordinary shares issued by the very biggest companies are often referred to as **blue chip** shares.

✔ A stock or share which is being offered with the dividend included is commonly referred to as being **cum-dividend**.

✔ A stock or share which is being offered with the dividend excepted is commonly referred to as being **ex-dividend**.

Chapter Two

Why Share Prices Fluctuate

*KEY FEATURE: We have all heard that, "shares can go down as well as up" but few people talk about exactly **why** share prices fluctuate. The purpose of this chapter is to throw a little light on the subject by taking a brief look at how the stock market works.*

SHARES ARE bought and sold on the stock market. This is - in theory - much like any other market; a place where buyers meet with sellers and deal-making is the order of the day. In a perfect world the only thing that should affect the price of shares is the performance of the companies which issue them. In reality the stock market is a little more complicated because demand for shares fluctuates from day to day due to a number of factors. These are:

- The general economic climate.
- The laws of supply and demand.
- The general mood of investors.

Each of these factors affects the stock market - and thus share prices - in different ways. To make these variable influences as easy as possible to understand, let us take a look at each one in turn...

The General Economic Climate

This is, to put it simply, the state of the country we live in from a financial point of view. The general economic climate is affected by wars, rumours of wars, unemployment figures, interest rates, current or pending political elections, the size of the national debt and a whole host of other imponderables. Unfortunately, few people ever really seem to agree as to what is, or is not, good for the economy.

For example, if the rate of unemployment increases dramatically, one group of doom-and-gloomers will predict the arrival of a new depression or recession. On the other hand, if the rate of unemployment decreases dramatically, another group of doom-and-gloomers will state that the economy is progressing too quickly and must be slowed down! So having said that, is unemployment good or bad for the economy?

This state of affairs is something which invariably baffles the new investor. What you should remember is; what the majority of investors *believe* about the economical climate often affects share prices more than the economy itself. For example, if the majority of investors are optimistic then more shares will be bought and prices will tend to rise.

By the same token, if the majority of investors are pessimistic then more shares will be sold and prices will tend to fall. This optimism and pessimism doesn't have to be based on any real economic data.

The Laws of Supply and Demand

The laws of supply and demand are the same in the stock market as they are in any other type of market. If there is a high demand for a certain product and supply is limited then prices will tend to rise, but if there is little demand for a product then prices will tend to fall.

Demand for certain types of shares tends to rise or fall according to how the underlying company performs. The shares of an established company which has good prospects for further growth or profitability will naturally be in higher demand than those of a company which is relatively new and has few prospects.

As with the general economic climate, what investors *believe* about the prospects of a company can affect share prices as much as any amount of hard data. Rumours that XYZ Cigarettes are to be successfully sued by a disgruntled smoker can send share prices plummeting because investors know that *if* the rumour is true, the cost of damages will affect the overall profitability of the company and open the floodgates for similar claims. Similarly, rumours that ABC Avionics are about to be awarded with a mammoth contract from NASA can send share prices through the roof, simply because investors know that *if* the rumour is true profitability is sure to take an upward turn.

The General Mood of Investors

We have already referred to the general mood of investors twice in the last few minutes, and it must be said that this is what generates the majority of share price fluctuations. Let's face it, if share prices were determined solely by hard economic or corporate data then they would be far more stable than they are in actuality. The fact that share prices often fluctuate wildly despite hard data is proof that emotion is king as far as the stock market is concerned.

Emotions are impossible to quantify and even more difficult to predict, but a good idea of what the majority of investors think can be gained by paying close attention to the financial headlines in newspapers or on television news bulletins. These are the headlines which will be seen, read or heard by millions of investors - both private and professional - and undoubtedly have at least some effect on the direction the stock market takes.

To explain this situation, let us use the analogy of sheep and a shepherd. It is a rather crude analogy, but it sheds a great deal of light on the subject of share price fluctuations.

If you consider the masses of private investors to be sheep and the financial media to be a shepherd then it becomes clear that whichever direction the shepherd chooses to travel in, the sheep will surely follow. Of course, there is always the odd black sheep who goes against the trend, but in the main mass psychology will out and so financial headlines tend to become self-fulfilling prophecies.

For example, if a major financial journalist states that share prices are too high and will undoubtedly take a dramatic tumble in the near future, millions of sheep-like investors will take those words as gospel and act on them instinctively. They will sweat all night, call their brokers at first light and sell their holdings as quickly as possible. Supply drops off quite suddenly and naturally share prices do take the tumble that was predicted.

At this point everyone is sure that the financial journalist is a genius - if not a prophet - and so when he announces that the tumble is over and share prices are about to rocket, everyone piles back into the stock market. Demand soars, supply is limited and so share prices rise. The prophet scores two out or two for accuracy.

Because mass psychology has such a large effect on the stock market as a whole, patterns of rises, declines and crashes tend to repeat themselves quite dramatically over the long term. Certain patterns have been named and can be recognised quite readily when one knows what to look for. Here are the "big three" patterns which all investors should be aware of.

The Bull Market

A bull market is one in which share prices are on an upward trend. Share prices may dip for a day or week or two, but the underlying trend is upwards - often into new,

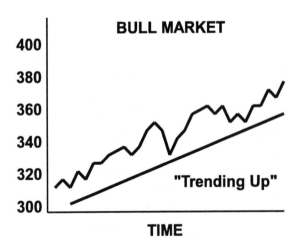

uncharted territory. The illustration below shows the share price of one imaginary company during a bull market. Note how the price goes down as well as up, but the overall trend is positive.

The average bull market lasts for around four years and general investing sentiment is usually quite positive. Although some of the more pessimistic "gurus" of the investing world will warn of the impending down-trend which is "inevitable" even in the early months of a bull market, the majority of investors take confidence in the upward trend and continue buying shares even when hard data suggests that they are too expensive.

Towards the end of a bull market, the overall Price Earnings Ratio (see Chapter Eight) tends to be very high and news of rising interest rates will have begun to hit the headlines. At this stage even good news has little further positive effect on share prices.

The Bear Market

A bear market is one in which share prices are on a downward trend. Share prices may rise for a day or week or two, but the underlying trend is undisputedly downwards. The illustration below shows the share price of one imaginary company during a bear market. Note how the price goes up as well as down, but the overall trend is negative.

The average bear market lasts for around one year and general investing sentiment is usually quite negative. There is almost always talk from some quarters of the "inevitable" rise which lies just around the corner, but most investors avoid get-

ting involved in the stock market through fear of suffering losses - even when hard data suggests that share prices are too low.

Towards the end of a bear market, the overall Price Earnings Ratio (see Chapter Eight) tends to be very low and interest rates may begin to fall. At this stage even bad news has little further negative effect on share prices.

The Crash

A crash is commonly defined as a sharp fall in general share prices which reduces the overall value of the stock market by ten per cent or more. This is more of an event than a trend, but it is suitable for discussion here because a crash tends to follow a definite pattern.

To begin with, a crash normally happens when the vast majority of the investment world least expects it. Share prices will normally have been on an upward trend for quite some time on both sides of the Atlantic, often breaking into new, uncharted territory. During this time there will naturally have been some talk of how the market is due a "correction" of some kind, but in the main investor confidence will have been high. "This time things are different," many will say in response to the doom-and-gloomers.

And then, quite suddenly, the market suffers a massive drop. This could be due to bad economic news or some other event, but whatever sparks the initial fall in share prices, panic sets in and everyone heads for the exit. The phone lines to brokers become jammed as everyone desperately attempts to sell stock which no-one wants to buy, and the fall spirals rapidly.

However disastrous a stock market crash might appear, historical data indicates that recovery comes relatively quickly. *It took only two years to recover from the infamous stock market crash of 1987*, and if you look at this event from a wider perspective of ten or even five years it is apparent that the crash was merely a large and necessary correction to stabilise what had been quite a dramatic upward trend.

As long as an investor is taking the long term view, a crash is really not the end of the world. In fact after a crash has taken place there are almost always a variety of excellent opportunities to buy shares at ridiculously low prices, giving the potential for even greater profits in future years.

To buy, or not to buy?

That really is the question. With all of this talk of share price fluctuations, mass psychology, bull trends, bear trends and stock market crashes you might be forgiven for thinking that the answer is not to buy any shares to being with. This is an attitude which many investors take, but in the long-term it is largely a self-defeating one. Consider the following:

● If you are actively investing in the stock market with a long term perspective then, although you may have to ride out a strong bear trend or perhaps even a crash, given time the probability is that your investments will recover and go on to make further profits.

● If you are deliberately avoiding stock market invest- ment then, although you automatically avoid bear trends and any crash which may take place, you will also miss out on strong bull trends which have tremendous power to multiply your money.

If this is not enough to dispel any fear of downward cycles which the stock market may suffer, then perhaps you should consider this: there are a handful of advanced investment techniques which allow the investor to make good potential profits during good times *and bad*. In fact there is even a method of *insuring* your investments against the effect of crashes and strong bear trends. We will discuss these methods and techniques in Chapter 10, but for now just remember that in order to win, you have to be in.

Summary

✔ Share prices fluctuate due to a number of factors, namely: the current economic climate, the laws of sup- ply and demand and the general mood of investors.

✔ Mass psychology often affects the fluctuation of share prices as much - if not more so - than any other factor.

✔ Because mass psychology has such a large effect on the stock market as a whole, patterns of rises, declines and crashes tend to repeat themselves quite dramatically over the long term.

✔ A bull market is one in which share prices are on an upward trend. Share prices may dip from time to time, but the underlying trend is upwards. The average bull market lasts for around four years.

✔ A bear market is one in which share prices are on a downward trend. Share prices may rise from time to time, but the underlying trend is downwards. The average bear market lasts for around one year.

✔ A crash is commonly defined as a sharp fall in general share prices which reduces the overall value of the stock market by ten per cent or more. Historical data indicates that recovery from a crash usually comes relatively quickly.

Chapter Three

Buying And Selling Shares

KEY FEATURE: *Buying and selling shares is not as complicated as many people think. This chapter is designed to make the whole process much easier to understand.*

PEOPLE BUY and sell shares for a wide variety of reasons. Some want to try and make their capital grow steadily over the long term but want a better return than they would get by putting their money into savings or deposit accounts. Others like the idea of investing in particular companies or sectors of companies due to a personal or professional interest in the same. Still others buy and sell shares simply because they like to speculate about - and hopefully profit from - market movements.

For whatever reason you wish to benefit from shares, you first have to buy them! Many high street banks offer a broker service whereby they will obtain or sell shares on behalf of their customers. For the occasional share investor this arrangement offers a lot in the way of convenience. All that is usually required is for the investor to complete a simple form which instructs the bank to buy or sell a specific number of shares in a certain company and then ensure that adequate funds are made available. This done, he can go home and get on with his life, secure in the knowledge that his bank will follow his instructions and buy or sell his shares accordingly.

Unfortunately, there are a number of down-sides to using a bank to buy or sell shares on a regular basis. These are as follows:

- The amount of commission and fees charged by banks for brokering services is often more than the amount charged by dedicated brokers. This is because share brokering is only one extra service as far as the bank is concerned, but a prime service as far as the broker is concerned.

- Buying and selling shares through a bank may be subject to a delay of anywhere between a few minutes and a few days. This means that the actual price of the share in question could go up or down before they are purchased or sold on behalf of the investor. Of course, this may work in the investors favour (such as when a share price rises before a sell instruction is carried out) but it can equally work against him (such as when a share price rises before a buy instruction is carried out.) Dedicated brokers, on the other hand, tend to work on a more immediate basis with instant share-dealing being quite a common facility.

- Banks offer a variety of services, but they are best at banking. This is what they know best simply because this is what they do the most. The main occupation of a dedicated broker, on the other hand, is dealing with shares. This means that a dedicated broker is almost always more knowledgeable about the subject and is therefore in a better position to pass this knowledge on to the investor.

If you intend to deal in shares on anything other than an occasional basis, you would do well to consider doing your business via a dedicated broker rather than through a bank. A broker can make share dealing faster, less expensive and (depending on the type of broker you choose) a whole lot easier.

There are two types of brokers available to private investors. These are traditional stockbrokers and execution-only stockbrokers.

A **traditional stockbroker** will give his client advice, recommendations and market pointers in addition to buying or selling on the client's behalf. This advice can be extremely valuable for investors who are new to the world of shares, and will often help them avoid some of the mistakes which beginners often make. Because traditional stockbrokers do more than just buy and sell, the commissions they charge tend to be slightly higher than those charged by execution-only brokers - an additional expense which is often a price worth paying.

An **execution-only stockbroker** does not give his client any advice, recommendations or market pointers. He simply acts as the middleman between the investor and the market, buying and selling on his clients behalf. Execution only brokers usually offer the lowest commissions of all, but investors must be prepared to make their own decisions and live by the results.

If you are fully conversant with financial jargon, and understand the field you want to invest in thoroughly, then an execution-only broker may well meet your needs. Otherwise it would be better to err on the side of caution and deal through a traditional broker who will help you take your first steps into the market.

Selecting either a traditional or execution-only broker is largely a matter of making a short-list, discussing your requirements (and theirs) with each and then opting for the one which will be most suitable to your needs. Many brokers advertise in the financial press and also in more general directories such as The Yellow Pages. If you can, you should obtain references from any other private investors you know, since personal experience of a broker will often tell you more than any number of glossy brochures or pamphlets.

Once you have a short-list of brokers to contact, you then need to have a brief discussion with each so that you can determine if they are able (and willing) to offer you the kind of service you require. The main questions you need to ask any broker you are considering are:

What type of new clients are they accepting, if any?

Some brokers will only accept new clients who intend to put substantial amounts of business their way. Others are more than happy to accept small private investors. Discovering at the outset whether the broker you are talking to would be willing to take on your business might save you a great deal in the way of wasted time.

What are your commission rates?

Don't beat around the bush when it comes to talking about money - after all, this is what brokers talk about all day long. Most brokers charge commission according to a sliding scale. This obviously means that the larger your investments are, the more commission you will pay. Almost all brokers establish a minimum commission fee which is payable on all transactions below a certain limit. Ask for both minimum commission details and sliding scale rates and this will help you to compare the broker with the others you contact.

Are there any other charges?

Often you won't need to ask this question because the broker will tell you about any additional fees when discussing commissions. If he doesn't, find out if he charges any management fees over and above the commission rates - most do. Some brokers who manage their clients portfolios set fees which are related to the performance of the portfolio they control. This motivates them to make the best returns they can, so if you are aiming to have a broker take care of your portfolio and make your decisions for you, a fee which is directly related to performance might be a good thing.

What is your track record?

Some brokers are better than others when it comes to making money grow. Ask about past performance and you will get some idea of how useful his advice is. Obviously, if you are looking for an execution-only broker then you should not ask this question because no advice will be given and so past performance does not exist.

Once you have telephoned a few brokers and possibly leafed through any brochures they send you, a decision can be made on the basis of the information you have accumulated. Ask around your friends and acquaintances and see if you know anyone who has any personal recommendations. You can take these recommendations into account before making a final decision. Finally, if you are still unsure about which broker to use, consider consulting a professional financial advisor.

Registering with a Broker

Once you have found a suitable broker which you would like to deal with, you must then register as one of his clients. Normally this will involve little more than completing a few application forms and sending the broker a cheque which he can then invest according to your instructions. Sometimes however - especially if you want your broker to make your investment decisions for you - an informal meeting may be suggested so that you can discuss your objectives and investment preferences more fully in person.

Buying and Selling

When you have arranged to use the services of a broker, you are then free to start buying and selling shares and put your knowledge into practice. The majority of reliable brokers accept buy and sell instructions over the telephone, and this is the most convenient way of share dealing for all parties.

From the investors point of view, buying and selling shares over the telephone has several distinct advantages over visiting a broker in person or dealing by one of the less common methods, such as by post:

- Telephone dealing is the most cost and time efficient method of dealing in shares. No travel is involved (except perhaps to the nearest telephone kiosk!) and no appointments are necessary.

- Telephone dealing allows the investor to take advantage of stock market fluctuations as quickly as possible.

This means that if the stock market begins to rise or fall dramatically, the investor can buy or sell shares in order to try and turn the trend into profit.

- Because a telephone call is so easy to make, an investor can usually contact his broker just to seek guidance (this service is not available from execution-only brokers) or information on his shares or prospective shares with no obligation to actually buy or sell.

- Telephone dealing allows investors to trade on either a short-term basis if that is what they wish to do. For example, an investor could buy shares in the morning, watch them rise and then sell them a few hours later, taking a welcome profit in the process.

  This is a more speculative approach to shares than many investors would like to take, but a growing number of people find this form of share dealing particularly fascinating - especially in volatile markets where profits (and it must be said, losses) can be made in a matter of hours.

Buying and selling shares over the telephone is a fairly simple matter and often takes just a few minutes. Once a decision has been reached about which shares an investor wants to buy or sell (according to his own knowledge or the advice of his broker) he is normally asked to give the broker the following information:

- His account number with the broker.

- The name (and type, if applicable) of the shares he wishes to deal in on this occasion.

●   His instructions as to whether he wishes to buy shares or sell existing ones.

●   The quantity of shares he wishes to buy or sell.

The broker may then tell the investor the 'price' at which the shares are trading and selling for, and ask if these are agreeable. This 'price' will be quoted as two figures, such as 100-104. The lower figure is the **bid quote** - an indication of how much will be paid to the investor for each share sold (100p). The higher figure is the **offer quote** - an indication of how much it will cost the investor to buy each share (104p). The difference between the two quoted figures is known as **the spread**.

It is important to realise that occasionally just one figure is given in newspapers and some other sources. This is known as the **mid-price** and is, as the term suggests, the mid point of the bid offer spread. The mid-price for the above quoted share would therefore be 102.

You should note that the share prices quoted are hardly ever guaranteed and can fluctuate even before the broker has a chance to hang up the telephone. The **striking price** (the price at which a shares deal is actually struck) may therefore differ from the prices quoted on the telephone. An investor can get around this fact by instructing his broker not to buy or sell above or below a particular price. This allows the investor to know for definite the maximum amount of money the deal will cost if executed.

Once all of these points have been confirmed (the telephone conversations to brokers are usually recorded in case a dispute arises) then that is all there is to it. The deal has been made. Within a few days the investor will receive a contract note, which is a written confirmation of his transaction and, presuming that this is correct, it may be filed to serve as a permanent record. Finally, if shares have been bought, a share certificate will be sent to the investor direct from the company registrars as legal proof of his purchase.

Buying and selling shares is not as complicated as many people tend to think. Once you have access to the services of a broker and understand the various prices and terms which are quoted, actually dealing is a simple matter of issuing appropriate instructions.

Summary

✔   If you intend to deal in shares on anything other than an occasional basis, you would do well to consider doing your business via a **dedicated broker**.

✔   There are two types of brokers available to private investors. These are **traditional** stockbrokers and **execution-only** stockbrokers.

✔   A traditional stockbroker will give his client **advice**, recommendations and market pointers in addition to buying or selling on the client's behalf.

✔   An execution-only stockbroker does not give his client any advice, recommendations or market pointers. He simply acts as the **middleman** between the investor and the market, buying and selling on his clients behalf.

✔ Selecting either a traditional or execution-only broker is largely a matter of making a short-list, discussing your requirements with each and then opting for the one which will be most suitable to your needs.

✔ Brokers often quote two figures to prospective investors. The lower figure is the **bid** quote - an indication of how much will be paid to the investor for each share sold. The higher figure is the **offer** quote - an indication of how much it will cost the investor to buy each share. The difference between the two quoted figures is known as the **spread**.

✔ The price at which the actual shares are bought or sold is known as the **striking price**.

Chapter Four

Unit and Investment Trusts

KEY FEATURE: Unit and Investment Trusts are investment vehicles which are designed to help the investor spread his risk and pool his financial resources with other investors.

SPREADING YOURSELF over a wide area is often the best way to avoid calamity. Consider a pond which is frozen over. If you need to reach something in the middle of the pond you can either walk across the ice and risk breaking through the surface, or you can lie down and slither towards the object. This second method has the effect of spreading your body weight fairly evenly over a larger area of ice, thus reducing the risk of the ice breaking underneath you.

This analogy works quite well in the world of stock market investment in that there are two main methods of trying to secure profits. You can either pour your money into just a few shares and hope that they are strong enough to help you make the profits you want, or you can spread your money over a broad variety of shares in order to spread risk and - hopefully - reduce the risk of losses.

Unfortunately, few private investors have the financial where-withal to invest in a wide range of companies and still stand a chance of achieving a good level of capital growth. Part of the reason being the costs involved with dealing. If you are starting with £10,000, then the most shares you can practicably invest in is around 10. Otherwise the cost of buying each set of shares will eat up a larger percentage of your original cash.

For this reason many people pool their financial resources by investing in a trust of some kind. This chapter discusses how this pooling of resources works, the types of pooled investments available and the pros and cons of each.

Unit Trusts

A Unit Trust is an investment vehicle in which money from a group of investors is pooled and used to create a diverse portfolio on their behalf. Each investor is allocated a number of units according to the size of his original investment and will receive the relevant proportion of profits after all costs and charges have been taken into consideration. To illustrate how this works in practice, consider the following example...

A trust invests £5 Million in a wide variety of stocks and securities. It splits this portfolio into 1,000 separate units. Each unit therefore costs £5,000.

The portfolio does well and the £5 Million grows to some £8 Million. Each unit is now worth £8,000 (£8m divided by 1,000 units = £8,000) and so any investor who bought a unit at the original price of £5,000 will have made £3,000 profit before charges. What is more, the individual investors have left all of the investment decisions and portfolio management to the unit trust company.

Individual investors can leave unit trusts at any time by selling their units, but this type of investment vehicle should primarily be seen as medium to long term investments. Similarly, investors can increase their holdings by purchasing further units whenever they want. The cost of units, however, will obviously rise and fall according to the performance of the trust itself.

The main advantages of investing in Unit Trusts are:

✔ An individual investor can spread his money over a much wider range of securities in a unit trust than would be possible if he built his own portfolio of shares (see Chapter 5). This is because the unit trust is a pool of money, and something like £5 Million from 1,000 separate investors can be spread more thinly than a much smaller individual fund of £5,000.

✔ Some unit trusts encourage investors by allowing people to invest small sums on a regular (usually monthly) basis as well as, or instead of, in lump sums. Thus it is possible to take advantage of a unit trust with an investment which can often be as small as £25 per month.

✔ Unit Trusts are handled by professional fund managers, so the individual investors do not have to make any specific portfolio management decisions.

Before deciding to get involved with any particular unit trust, you must bear in mind that different unit trusts will have different performance records. Some unit trusts have done extremely well in the past whilst others have not done so well. Of course, past performance cannot be taken as a guarantee of what might happen in the future. But large investment houses employ teams of people to manage the trust's assets and these teams build up certain investment know-how which will not disappear overnight. So it makes sense that you should look to join a winning team if you decide to join one at all.

Investment Trusts

These are companies which exist specifically for the purpose of investing in other companies. Like most other large companies, they issue shares and are quoted on the stock market in their own right.

The main difference between a unit trust and an investment trust from the investors point of view is that an investment trust has a greater number of options as far as generating profits are concerned. As well as investing in the shares of other quoted companies, an investment trust may also:

● Buy shares in unquoted companies

● Generate money by investing in derivative products (see Chapter 10)

● Invest in property

● Borrow money for investment purposes

In fact, an investment trust can virtually generate money in whatever way it chooses, within certain limits. This is because, unlike a unit trust, it is a company in its own right and not merely a pool of money.

Another difference is the fact that unit trusts are **open-ended**, whilst investment trusts are **closed-ended**. This means that once all the shares in an investment trust have been sold, no more will be made available. Unit trusts, on the other hand, can take in as much 'new' money as it wishes.

The fact that more shares in an investment trust will not be issued creates price fluctuations as demand rises and falls - just like any other share. Unit trusts, however, fluctuate in price depending on the value of the shares owned by the trust. investment trusts are normally valued every month, whilst unit trust values are calculated daily.

Investing in an investment trust is a simple matter of buying its shares. Some investment trusts go even further and set up a savings plan whereby investors can benefit from their abilities with either monthly or lump-sum investments. Investment trusts which offer a monthly savings facility are very popular with people who are new to the idea of stock market investment, but - as always - professional financial advice is recommended before a decision to get involved is made.

Personal Equity Plans

Personal Equity Plans (commonly referred to as PEPs) were launched in 1986 by the Chancellor of the Exchequer. They allow individuals to invest a certain amount each year (the investment limit fluctuates) and enjoy exemption from tax on both capital gains and interest payments. There are two main types of Personal Equity Plan available, and these are as follows:

The General PEP allows the individual to invest in a variety of shares in order to help spread risk. The companies which are to be invested in can either be chosen by the individual investor using a *Self-Select PEP*, or can be chosen by the PEP manager. The latter option would be most suited to those individuals who wish to benefit from a general PEP but who don't particularly want to follow the stock market and make their own selections.

The Single Company PEP allows the individual to invest in one company only. Some single company PEPs allow the investor to change the company he invests in, but often a charge is levied if this facility is used.

Although a PEP is not a pooled investment vehicle, it can often contain pooled investments such as unit or investment trusts. This can make them particularly attractive to smaller investors who want to make the most out of a PEP's tax benefits.

Personal Equity Plans must be managed by an approved professional, and this means that management charges are passed on to the investor. If the investor pays little or no tax he should therefore decide if these charges are worth paying, since he will not benefit a great deal from the tax breaks which PEPs offer.

For other investors who would normally pay a higher amount of tax on their investments and have not already taken advantage of the facility, PEPs can be a godsend. They do however have to be thought about carefully before any firm investment decision is made. Remember that a bad investment is a bad investment, whether it is tax efficient or not!

Conclusion

Pooling your finances with those of other investors can be an excellent way of spreading stock market risk without having to invest a large amount of money. As with all investment vehicles, some pooled investments perform better than others, but in the main they are a valuable alternative to taking an unwanted risk in just one or two shares.

Summary

✔ Spreading yourself over a wide area is often the best way to avoid calamity, and that is the basic principle on which unit and investment trusts are built.

✔ A **Unit Trust** is an investment vehicle in which money from a group of investors is pooled and used to create a diverse portfolio on their behalf.

✔ An **Investment Trust** is a company which exists specifically for the purpose of investing in other companies. Investment Trusts issue their own shares and are quoted on the stock market in their own right.

✔ A **Personal Equity Plan** (PEP) allows individuals to invest a certain amount each year and enjoy exemption from tax on both capital gains and interest payments.

✔ A **General PEP** allows the individual to invest in a variety of shares in order to help him spread his risk.

✔ A **Single Company PEP** allows the individual to invest in one company only.

Chapter Five

Building a Share Portfolio

KEY FEATURE: A portfolio is a varied collection of investments which through diversity give a certain element of stability. They are usually built with a specific objective in mind.

THE LAST chapter explained that the best way to reduce the risk of calamity is to spread your investments over a wide area. It also said that pooled investments can help an individual to take this approach and diversify his share-holdings.

Pooled investments, however, are not the only way of spreading risk. Given adequate investment capital you can build your own portfolio of shares which balances higher-risk holdings with those of lower risk. By doing this you hope to achieve steady long-term capital growth without having all of your eggs in one basket.

For example, Mr Wynne wants to invest in shares in order to help him prepare for retirement in ten years time. He has £50,000 to invest, so he could build a portfolio of shares which would offer him good returns and good security at the same time. He could split his £50,000 into perhaps twenty

separate funds of £2,500 and make twenty different investments - some in blue-chip shares for security and some in new
issues for higher potential gains.

By spreading his total portfolio capital of £50,000 over twenty
different investments, Mr Wynne would effectively be spreading his risks. If a handful of shares go down, others may increase in value and so offset the loss. If he had invested the
whole £50,000 into just one company, however, the loss could
be catastrophic. Of course this is a highly simplistic view of
how a portfolio works, but it does serve to illustrate how portfolios can be used to help spread risks quite thinly.

A well diversified portfolio can help to give your investments
a general balance between risk and reward, but diversification
can also help to smooth any delays between the interest payments you receive on your individual holdings.

Of course, it would be foolish for any investor to put all of his
money in shares. A share portfolio should be just one part of a
larger financial plan. This larger financial plan should be or-
ganised so that a careful balance of low-, medium- and high-
risk investments is maintained at all times. This approach
(called *The Pyramid Principle*) is explained in more detail in
Understand Bonds and Gilts in a Day, but the principles are
well worth repeating here.

The Pyramid Principle states that the investments of any
individual or organisation should be set up in such a way
so that there is a balance of risk. There should be three
sections to this investment pyramid - a wide foundation of
very secure, low yield investments, a smaller mid-section
of medium risk, medium reward investments and an even

smaller peak of higher risk investments which give the potential for even higher gains. The pyramid would therefore look something like this:

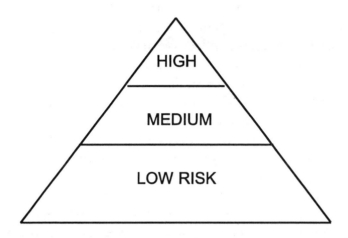

The purpose of The Pyramid Principle is to try and ensure that no investor - either private or corporate - becomes "top heavy" by taking on a lot of high risk investments without first having a solid base and mid-section of low and medium risk investments. Let's look at these three sections of low, medium and high risk in turn and see how they apply to the share investor.

Low Risk Base

This is money which is as secure as can be. National Savings, deposit accounts and TESSA's fall into this range. These vehicles generally offer only small potential rewards but give the investor a very good element of capital safety. Fixed interest stocks would fall into this category because they are loans rather than purchases of equity, so the risk of losing money is fairly low.

No investor should contemplate taking on medium or high risks until he has first built a dependable low risk base of capital which - although probably not earning a great deal - can be relied on whatever the markets may be doing.

Medium Risk Mid-Section

Medium risk investments are those which offer more potential rewards but still leave most of the capital fairly secure. Personal Equity Plans and Unit Trusts are generally said to be in this range. So are blue chip shares issued by solid, reliable companies which are least likely to go into liquidation and are likely to show good profits over the long term.

The Medium risk section of the pyramid is designed to give the investor a higher level of return without taking very big risks. Again, until you have built this section of your pyramid you shouldn't get involved in the next level, which are high-risk investments.

High Risk Peak

High risk investments include derivatives (see Chapter Ten), penny shares (see Chapter Six) and others which give the potential - though certainly not a promise - for extremely high rewards. This high-risk peak should only be built when the earlier sections of your pyramid have been established. Investing in high-risk investments before that point could ruin you financially if things go wrong.

Going back to our example of Mr Wynne; a good application of The Pyramid Principle might be for him to have fifty per cent of his money in lower-risk deposit accounts or National

Savings, forty per cent in a medium risk share portfolio and just ten per cent in derivatives, penny shares and other high-risk investments. If this happened, the share portfolio would, when illustrated graphically, sit in the medium-risk mid-section of the pyramid structure, as follows:

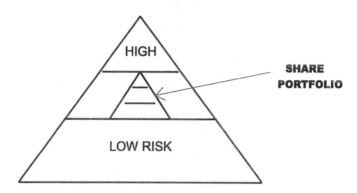

For a share portfolio to be effective, it should be designed with a specific aim in mind. This will help to clarify the investors position at any given moment and adjust the portfolio as and when it becomes necessary. Here we will take a look at a specific financial goals of accumulating long-term savings, and consider how a share portfolio might help this goal to achieved...

Long Term Savings

We all have things that we would like to purchase in the future, and we have future event which need to be planned for if they are to be paid for. A share portfolio can help to finance these purchases and/or events if it is geared for capital growth over the long term. What's more, the portfolio can be built according to the desired risk level of the investor.

● For the investor who wants to take a relatively low level of risk, a suitable portfolio might mix a good proportion of fixed-interest stocks with a few hand-picked blue-chip shares to help boost potential gains.

● For the investor who wants to take a medium risk in order to achieve his goals, a suitable portfolio might focus on a variety of blue-chip shares which, although unlikely to generate vast profits, are equally unlikely to lose their value quite so quickly as higher-risk shares.

● For the investor who would like to take a higher level of risk, a suitable portfolio could focus on new issues which have the potential for greater profits and counter-balance these with more stable blue-chip shares.

Sleeves up and hands on

It is vitally important that all investors see their portfolios as highly flexible organisms which can and should be adapted to suit any changing economic situations and/or any change in the desired risk level. The investor should review the performance of his or her portfolio on an annual basis at the very least to ensure that it is on target to meet the pre-determined goals. If it is not then the portfolio should be thoroughly revised and under-performing shares should be sold in favour of those that hold more promise. Of course, the balance of risk and reward must continue to be maintained.

If you are not willing to roll up your sleeves and take a hands-on approach to maintaining your portfolio then you should leave this to someone else. You could either employ the services of a professional portfolio manager or, alternatively, invest your money in a unit or investment trust.

When all is said and done, building and maintaining a well-balanced portfolio is one of the best ways for an investor to spread his risk without having to pool resources or call on the services of a professional. Of course, managing a portfolio properly involves being able to value the shares within it, monitor stock market movements and then act appropriately. To help you decide if this is something you wish to do for yourself, there is a discussion of professional methods for share evaluation and analysis later in the book.

Summary

✔ A portfolio is a varied collection of investments which, through **diversity**, give a certain element of **stability**. Most portfolios are built with a specific objective in mind.

✔ A well diversified portfolio can help give your investments a general balance between **risk and reward**.

✔ Portfolios should be **well balanced** and follow the pyramid structure, mixing low, medium and higher risk investments.

✔ You should **review** the performance of your portfolio on an annual basis at the very least to ensure that it is on target to meet your goals.

✔ Managing a portfolio properly involves being able to value the shares within it, **monitor stock market movements** and then act appropriately.

Chapter Six

Penny Shares

KEY FEATURE: A Penny Share is commonly said to be one which has a low price in relation to the broader market.

IF ANY INVESTOR wants to know why penny shares are seen by many people as being one of the most exciting types of shares, he need look no further than to the example of Polly Peck in the early 1980's. Shares in this company were available for just 9p each at one time, but three years later they were valued at an incredible £35. This means that a £900 investment in the original penny shares grew to some £350,000 - a mammoth profit by anyone's standards.

You might be forgiven for thinking that this was a one-off, but you would be wrong. Although dramatic increases in value don't happen every day, there have been many cases where a 12p penny share has grown to a value of £10, or a 20p share to a value of £30

It should go without saying that the most attractive thing about penny shares is the seemingly unlimited growth potential you can enjoy when you pick a real winner. They are, however, high-risk investments which are only suitable if you are prepared to lose - in a worse case scenario - every penny of your investment. This is only likely to happen if you let a losing investment ride on to the bitter end. If you cut any losses quickly and let profits continue their run, you stand at least a decent chance of penny share success. But a **chance** is not a **guarantee**, and so penny shares are most definitely not suitable for the faint-hearted.

What gives penny shares their potential?

It might seem odd that a share costing less than a daily newspaper could triple or quadruple its value in a short while, whilst a share costing many times more may only grow a little over the same period. But if you look at the matter closely the apparent paradox is quite easy to understand.

Consider a share in a blue-chip company. The company has been around for years and has grown from a small-time producer of widgets to the world's leading brand. It has expanded all it can, and there is little room for further growth. All it can really hope for is that widgets become more popular and that this popularity helps to increase the market demand for their products still further.

A penny share company is an entirely different proposition. The company is likely to be fairly new and relatively small. Its product may not yet have caught the public eye, and many people won't even have heard of the company itself. From this point the company can usually do one of two things:

● Fail and fall into even further obscurity, if not out of business altogether.

● Succeed and grow at a relatively dramatic rate.

Obviously, if the company fails then even the penny shares will fall in value. Occasionally a penny share can become virtually worthless in these situations simply because there are few people willing to buy them. But if the company succeeds and perhaps lands an important contract which increases the interest of more "mainstream" investors, then the share price can easily double, treble, quadruple and go on to create massive gains for its early penny share investors.

Therefore a penny share has more **potential** for profits simply because the company which issues it tends to have more potential for growth, expansion and greater success in the business world.

High risk, high reward?

Penny shares are high-risk, high reward investments and definitely not for the faint-hearted. But whilst this may technically be true, the risk and reward ratio should be examined in greater detail, since there are benefits to investing in penny shares which most people overlook.

To begin with, the potential losses on a penny share investment are always known at the outset. If you buy 1,000 shares at 10p then you could - if the bottom dropped out of the world - lose £100. Whilst this loss is a seemingly frightening one hundred per cent of your initial investment, it is often not near as much as you might lose on a blue-chip investment should things go wrong. For example, if you buy 1,000 shares at £1.50 and the share price falls by ten per cent, your original investment of £1,500 will now only be worth £1,350. Thus a ten per cent fall on a blue chip share can often damage your pocket more than a total loss on a penny share.

Looking at the situation from the other side of the fence, the potential gains from a penny share can be enormous. The glowing example of Polly Peck is a case in point. Just £90 invested in PP shares at 9p each would have grown to £3,500 just three years later. Compare this enormous return with what you might gain out of a blue-chip investment over the same period and the difference is clear.

Of course, no one would suggest that an investor should focus entirely on penny shares unless they really are prepared to ride the rough with the smooth. Adding a few penny shares to a more conservative portfolio would, however, give the potential for greater returns without breaking the bank should they fail to meet expectations.

Selecting penny shares

Succeeding with penny shares is simply a matter of picking the winners and avoiding the losers. Of course, this is easier said than done, but there are a couple of pointers which you might like to consider:

● Most penny share experts agree that assets are the most important consideration when looking for winners. The more assets a company has (in the form of property, machinery, etc.) the better.

Occasionally you will find shares which are worth less than the actual assets of the company, so if the worst happened and the liquidators moved in, there would be more than enough money generated by the sale of these assets to cover your original outlay - and perhaps a bit more besides.

● Technical analysis (see Chapter Nine) may help to provide clues about possible winners. But with penny shares in particular it is important to pay equal attention to more fundamental analysis, such as the amount of money the company has in the bank, etc.

If you are serious about wanting to tap into the potential of penny shares you would undoubtedly benefit greatly by studying some of the excellent books available on the subject. Some companies also issue tip-sheets and newsletters which are designed to highlight probable winners and losers.

Make no mistake, penny shares are more **volatile** than the average blue-chip shares which make headlines. But this volatility has helped some investors to make gargantuan profits in the past and the same is likely to happen in the future. If you are prepared to take a higher level of risk in the hope of making a potentially higher gain, penny shares may be worth their weight in gold.

Summary

A Penny Share is commonly said to be one which has a low price in relation to the broader market.

✔ Penny shares are high-risk investments which are only suitable if you are prepared to lose - in a worse case scenario - every penny of your investment. Of course, the same caution should be applied to all shares.

✔ The main advantage of penny shares is that their value can multiply many times over in a relatively short time.

Chapter Seven

Reading The Financial Press

KEY FEATURE: *The financial press is a valuable source of information which no serious or aspiring investor can afford to overlook. Knowing how to get the most out of the valuable resource can be a major key to your long-term success.*

THE DIFFERENCE between success and failure in any venture is often the quality of information at hand, and share investment is no exception to this general rule. The more you know about the share market, the shares available and the companies which issue them, the greater your chances of long term success.

The best source of share-related information can be found in financial publications such as the *Financial Times* and *Investors Chronicle*, but other daily newspapers also carry a substantial amount of share price information. In addition to specific company and share information, specialist financial publications also feature many articles and news snippets about general economic items which can be of enormous use.

This chapter will take a brief look at the main items of interest to any share investor, and in doing so, illustrate how you can get the most out of the financial press...

Headlines

It has already been said that the majority of investors are like sheep who act on herd instincts, buying or selling according to what everyone else is doing. The headlines in the financial press are one of the factors which affect this mass psychology in the first place, so you must pay attention to what they are saying.

It is obvious that not all headlines will agree, but again, the majority tends to rule. If seven out of ten headlines state that the stock market is heading for a crash then roughly seven out of ten people will believe this to be so and act on that belief as though it was a foregone conclusion. They will therefore tend to sell their shares rather than buy any more. Conversely, if the majority of headlines predict a stock market boom then you might expect the majority of investors to be more interested in buying than in selling.

Studying the headlines of the financial press can help you gauge what the majority of investors will be thinking during any given period, and thus give you an insight into how the stock market will react.

Share Prices

The closing prices of specific shares are central statistics which no investor can afford to ignore. They allow you to keep track of which shares are rising and which shares are falling, and are vital if you intend to use **Technical Analysis** (see Chapter Nine) to help you make your investment decisions.

Typically, shares are listed in groups, according to which sector of the market they are associated with. For example, television broadcasting companies and record companies tend to be listed under a heading such as "MEDIA" whilst computer manufacturing companies and retailers tend to be listed under "ELECTRICALS" or something similar. Knowing this can help you find the shares you are interested in quickly without having to wade through pages of listings.

The share details themselves normally comprise of at least five components, which are:

● The name of the company issuing the shares.

● The current share price.

● The change from the previous trading day.

● The share price high.

● The share price low.

This data might be set out as follows:

	Price	Change	Hi	Lo
Invisible Widgets	303	+7	303	270

This would mean that:

1) The ordinary shares issued by a company called Invisible Widgets stand at 303p each. This is the **mid-price**, so if you were to buy these shares they may actually cost a little more (say 305p), and if you were to sell them you may get back a

little less (say 301p). Share prices given in any publication are for informational purposes only, and errors and omissions do occur, so you must always check the prices with your broker before buying or selling.

2) The next item of data tells you that the shares rose by 7p on the day. This means that the previous days closing mid-price must have been 296p per share.

3) The third item tells you that the highest the shares have been is 303p per share. So Invisible Widgets' shares are currently trading at their highest level.

4) The final item tells you that the lowest the shares have been is 270p per share.

Sometimes other data is given, such as the *open, day hi* and *day lo* figures. These are simply the prices of the shares when the market opened and at the highest and lowest points on a particular day.

Investment Tips

A lmost every newspaper prints investment "tips" of one kind or another. These are buy or sell suggestions for certain shares and attract a massive following despite the fact that they are not to be construed as financial advice in the real sense of the phrase. Indeed, so many people follow the investment tips of particular publications that they too can tend to become **self-fulfilling prophecies**.

For example, if a tip is published in a popular Sunday newspaper to buy shares in Ocepoc Media Plc, millions of people will read that tip and thousands will act on it. The number of people who actually buy the shares will depend largely on how much the tipster is respected by the investing public, but you can be fairly sure that the share price will rise, at least for a short time, simply because of all the new buyers which the tip has generated. Similarly, a sell tip can cause the price of the share in question to fall over the next day or two.

Knowing what has been tipped as a buy or sell in the financial pages can be worth its weight in gold to the speculative investor who aims to generates profits by predicting share price movements, but that will be discussed further in Chapter Ten.

Director Dealings

It makes sense that the people who are intimately involved with a particular company are likely to know more about it than the average investor. For this reason, many publications print a list of the most notable "Director Dealings". These are the shares bought or sold by directors of the company in question, and they reveal whether the people actually running the company are happy to increase their investment in it or are looking to reduce their holdings.

Director Dealings
Ocepoc Plc	£350,000

Here, £350,000 has been invested by the director(s) in our fictitious company Ocepoc Plc. To many investors this is a significant transaction and could suggest that the director knows something that they don't in order to warrant such a large investment. Some private investors will therefore take a closer look at this company with a view to jumping aboard the band wagon and getting a slice of the action themselves.

Note the phrase, "a closer look" in that last paragraph. To buy or sell shares based solely on director dealings would be foolish. But such dealings, whether they are positive or negative, can and should be followed up with further study of the company in question. If this study concludes that the shares are indeed worth buying or selling, then the investor can act on this informed opinion.

Results Due

Almost all financial publications print a list of companies which are due to publish their final (annual) or interim (usually six monthly) accounts. Sometimes they also include an estimate of how much they think the **Earnings Per Share** (EPS) are likely to be.

Knowing which companies are due to publish their results is, in itself, of little importance. But if this schedule is read in conjunction with the table of Director Dealings, the investor can often put two and two together and come up trumps.

For example, if you have noted that a director of Ocepoc Plc has purchased £350,000 worth of shares in the last week, and that this company is due to publish its annual results next week, you might conclude that good news is on the horizon. This might explain why the director has made such a large investment, because if the results are good, he knows that the world and his wife will want to buy shares in his company, thus pushing the price up. By purchasing £350,000 of shares before the publication of the results, he can benefit from this increase in share price almost automatically.

Of course, if the director had sold £350,000 of shares, then you might conclude that the results may not be very good. In this case it is likely that the director has sold his shares because he thinks they will soon go down in value.

Again, you are dealing here with clues to, not promises of, what might happen in the future. It is always advisable to take financial advice before making any investment decision, particular if you are new to the stock market.

Make no mistake, learning how to read the financial press properly will allow you to take **full advantage** of what is, after all, a very economical resource. Begin paying attention to headlines, share prices, investment tips, director dealings and results due tables and you will find that, with a little practice, you can piece these items together like a jigsaw to provide a very comprehensive picture of the market as a whole.

Summary

✔ The **financial press** is a valuable source of information which no serious or aspiring investor can afford to overlook.

✔ **Headlines** in the financial press are one of the factors which affect this mass psychology of investors, so you must pay attention to what they are saying.

✔ Share prices allow you to keep **track** of which shares are rising and which shares are falling, and are vital if you intend to use Technical Analysis to help you make your investment decisions.

✔ **Investment tips** are followed by thousands of people and, at the very least, can often be seen as self-fulfilling prophecies.

✔ **Director Dealings** are printed in most financial publications and these can give you some insight as to what may lie in store for a company - particularly if they are studied in conjunction with a Results Due table.

Chapter Eight

Share Valuation

> *KEY FEATURE: Share Valuation techniques allow the investor to compare one share with others of a similar nature.*

Because the dividends payable on a share tend to fluctuate from year to year, and because the risks involved in holding a share are often unquantifiable, there is no exact method of finding out, in absolute terms, precisely how much an investor stands to make or lose by purchasing shares in a particular company.

There are, however, a number of share valuation techniques which investors can use to compare one share with others. These provide the investor with a rough guide to value rather than with absolute valuations. But a ball-park valuation is better than no valuation at all, so these techniques are used almost universally by professional and astute private investors alike.

There are three main techniques for evaluating a specific share, and these produce something called the Dividend Yield, P/E Ratio and Net Asset Value figures. Taking each calculation method in turn...

The Dividend Yield

The purpose of the dividend yield calculation is to help you determine how much income you are likely to receive from a particular share. There are two types of dividend yield calculation: an historic yield calculation and a prospective yield calculation.

The **historic yield** calculation is based on actual previous dividend payments. By basing the calculation on 'real' past data, an investor can determine quite accurately how much he or she stands to receive if future dividends are roughly equal in size to the ones which have already been paid.

The **prospective yield** calculation is more speculative in nature and is based on educated estimates regarding the size of future dividend payments.

Of course, neither the historic nor the prospective yield calculation can produce figures which are one hundred per cent reliable. This is because the value of a share is intrinsically linked to the value of the company which issues it. Unless you have a crystal ball and have been blessed with the gift of second sight, no one can really tell what the future has in store for any particular company. Having said that, if one assumes that past performance will be repeated - at least to some extent - in the future, the yield calculations can be extremely enlightening.

Because investors receive dividend payments after basic rate tax has been deducted, the first step in calculating the historic yield is to add this back on. To do this, use the following formula:

(Net Dividend / (100-current basic rate of tax)) x 100 = Gross Dividend

For example, if the net dividend for a certain share was 20p, and the basic rate of tax was 20 per cent, our calculation would be:

$$(20p / (100 - 20)) \times 100$$
$$(20p / 80) \times 100$$
$$0.25p \times 100 = 25p$$

Now that you know the historic gross dividend, you can calculate how much this is as a percentage of the share. To do this, simply divide the gross dividend by the price per share and multiply by one hundred.

For example, if our 25p gross dividend was received on a share which cost £7 (700p) then the dividend yield expressed as a percentage would be:

$$25p / 700p = 0.035$$
$$0.035 \times 100 = 3.5\%$$

Calculating prospective dividend yield is even easier, because since you are simply estimating future dividends, you might as well estimate the gross dividend straight away. For example, if you know that historically a gross dividend has been around 25p per share, and the company has forecast that future dividends are expected to be fifty per cent higher, you can reasonably estimate that the gross dividend will be around 37.5p per share. Armed with that projected figure, you can then calculate how much this is as a percentage of the share itself. Again, to do this, simply divide the gross dividend by the price per share and multiply by one hundred.

For example, if the share price is still 700p, the dividend as a percentage would be:

$$37.5p / 700p = 0.053$$
$$0.053 \times 100 = 5.3\%$$

Using Dividend Yield Figures

So much for calculating dividend yield figures - how do you actually use them? Well, there are two major ways of using the figures to help you make your investment decisions, and they are:

1 - To help balance a portfolio of shares

If your portfolio is already heavily geared to high-yield dividends which could have little potential in the way of capital growth, you may want to balance these with shares which have smaller dividend yields but which have a larger potential for future capital growth, and vice versa.

For example, if you have shares in a lot of blue chip companies, the dividend yields may be quite high, but because these companies are already well established, there is little room for potential expansion and the share price itself may not increase very much. Shares in a smaller company, although producing smaller dividends, might well have the potential to double or perhaps even triple in value over a number of years as the company expands. By balancing lower-yields with the higher ones your portfolio should also provide a good balance between income and capital growth when viewed over the medium to long term.

2 - To compare shares within the same market sector

If you are of the opinion that one particular market sector will do well over the next few years, you can calculate the dividend yields of the major players in this sector and decide which of them is most suited to your investment needs.

For example, if you think that the electrical retail sector is likely to experience a surge in profits, you could calculate the dividend yields for the top ten companies in this sector and then decide which share offers, in your opinion, the best potential for either income or capital growth.

It should go without saying that dividend yields should not be blindly used to help you choose shares. Basing any investment decision on pure mathematics is never to be advised. However, dividend yield figures can be a valuable aid in making investment decisions.

The Price Earnings Ratio

The Price Earnings Ratio (often called the P/E Ratio) is most commonly used when the desired outcome is a direct comparison of profits between two or more companies. It indicates the relationship between the share price and the profit potential of the company which issues it.

Before you can begin to calculate the price earnings ratio itself, you must first calculate how much of the company earnings are available for shareholders. You do this by dividing after-tax profits by the total number of shares issued by the company.

For example, if a company has 50,000 shares in issue and profits, after the deduction of corporation tax, are £25,000, then our calculation would be:

$$£25,000 / 50,000 = 50p$$

This is the amount of money which each share has theoretically earned during the year in question. It is "theoretical" because although all earned profits belong to the shareholders, some will undoubtedly be re-invested back into the company to fund expansion, and so on.

Once you have this figure, you can calculate the price earnings ratio as follows:

Share Price / Earned profits per share = Price Earnings Ratio

If the price of the fictitious share is £3 then the calculation would be:

$$300p / 25p = 12$$

This is what is known as an *historic* price earnings ratio, because it is based on precise historical data (company profits after tax, share price, etc.) As with dividend yields, it is also possible to produce a *prospective* price earnings ratio, but this is vastly more complicated and relies on accurate forecasting of such data. Unfortunately, such forecasting is seldom accurate, so the prospective price earnings ratios themselves tend to be less useful than one might initially think.

Using Price Earnings Ratio Figures

P/E ratios are most commonly used when the desired outcome is a direct comparison of profits between two or more companies. Obviously for such a comparison to be made accurately, the investor must ensure that the price earnings ratio for each company is calculated over the same period. It is also a good idea to keep Price Earnings Ratio comparisons to companies which trade in the same country and even the same business sector. This is because a comparison between two or more companies which operate in different economical climates will almost undoubtedly be more difficult to interpret.

Interpreting Price Earnings Ratios is just as much of an art (some would say more so) than it is a science. This is because no two companies are absolutely identical and this in itself will cause at least some ratio discrepancy. Large discrepancies, however, may be more significant.

Consider two companies which are very similar. One has a Price Earnings Ratio of nine and the other a ratio of 15. In this situation, the discrepancy could indicate any of the following:

● The shares of the first company are not as high as they ought to be. This would mean that they may be good value investments.

● The shares of the second company are higher than they ought to be. This would indicate that they may not be so good from an investment point of view.

● The discrepancy is caused by some factor you have not yet considered. Perhaps the companies are not as similar as you first thought.

Now obviously it is necessary to study each company in further detail before any one of these conclusions can be reached with any confidence. Using the Price Earnings Ratio has, however, given you something to focus on and is a good way of making initial, if sometimes rather crude comparisons.

Net Asset Value

One question which many prospective investors in a company want to know the answer to is this: If the bottom dropped out of the world and the company in question went into liquidation, how much might a shareholder reasonably expect to receive?

The Net Asset Value calculation is designed to answer this question. It works by dividing the total assets allocated to shares by the number of shares which have been issued (found by subtracting short- and long-term liabilities, provisions and charges from the published net asset figure).

For example, if a company has £3000 million pounds for ordinary shares and there are 1500 million ordinary shares in circulation, the Net Asset Value would be:

£3,000,000,000 divided by 1,500,000,000 = £2 per share

In other words, for every ordinary share held, the shareholder could reasonably expect to receive £2 should the company cease trading. This figure can help the investor to decide if investing in a particular company is compatible with the amount of risk they are prepared to take. For example, a low-risk investor would probably want to concentrate on companies which have higher Net Asset Value figures, whereas a more adventurous investor might be prepared to invest in companies with lower Net Asset Value figures.

Because so many investors are interested in Net Asset Value figures, many companies include them in their accounts. It may not always be necessary, therefore, to calculate the figures for yourself.

No share valuation calculation can ever be one hundred per cent accurate and they should **never** be followed blindly. Having said that, the figures provided by the calculations we have outlined in this chapter can often provide good **clues** as to whether or not a particular investment might be suited to your needs.

Summary

✔ There are a number of share valuation techniques which investors can use to **compare** one share with others of a similar nature.

✔ The **dividend yield** calculation is designed to help you determine how much income you are likely to receive from a particular share.

✔ The **Price Earnings Ratio** (often called the P/E Ratio) is designed to indicate the relationship between the price of a share and the profit potential of the company which issues it.

✔ The **Net Asset Value** (NAV) calculation is designed to indicate how much a shareholder might reasonably expect to receive should the company cease trading and go into liquidation.

Chapter Nine

Technical Analysis

KEY FEATURE: Technical analysis is the art of predicting whether a financial market or share price will rise or decline according to the interpretation of charted historical data.

NOW THIS might sound rather complex, but in its basic form technical analysis is really quite straightforward, and anyone with a little time can use it to help them pick probable investment winners.

There are a huge number of technical analysis indicators used by investors and many are beyond the scope of this book. Instead *Understand Shares in a Day* will limit itself to the main indicators and you will learn how to use them yourself with little more than a few sheets of graph paper, a small sample of historical share or market data and a calculator.

The Moving Average

This is the most popular technical indicator in use, and it is one which is employed by small-time private investors and professional corporate investors alike. The idea is to chart a sample of past closing prices (that is the price of a specific share or index at the close of business each day) and then superimpose a moving average which is the sum of previous prices divided by the number of days used.

The idea is that when the two resulting charted lines cross, a buy or sell signal is generated. This specific analysis method will be described in detail in a few moments, but first you need to know how the chart is created step-by-step. For the purposes of example consider the share price movements of a fictitious company called Talking Widgets Plc.

Step One - Obtain the Data

The first step is to obtain a sample of **historical data**. As indicated, most daily newspapers have a financial page which will tell you the closing price of the most popular shares for the previous trading day, but if you wish to chart a more unusual share or commodity then you may need to refer to a specialist newspaper such as *The Financial Times*. Alternatively, a lot of financial information is given on *Teletext*. Whatever medium you use to obtain your data, the information you need is the closing price of the share you are interested in.

The amount of data you collect will depend on what type of investment signals you are looking for. It is generally agreed among investment professionals that short moving averages will give short-term buy and sell signals, whilst longer moving averages will give longer-term buy and sell signals.

For the purposes of this illustration you can construct a seven day moving average to provide short-term buy and sell signals, since the basic principle is exactly the same regardless of how much data is actually used. You therefore begin by obtaining the closing price of Talking Widgets Plc shares for the past seven days. Let's assume that they read as follows:

Day 1	360
Day 2	370
Day 3	394
Day 4	380
Day 5	385
Day 6	387
Day 7	395

Step Two - Draw up a Chart

Once you have the necessary data, you can then draw up a chart so that the prices are given in diagramattical form. The date of each price should be given on the horizontal axis and the closing price should be indicated on the vertical axis. A completed chart would therefore look something like this:

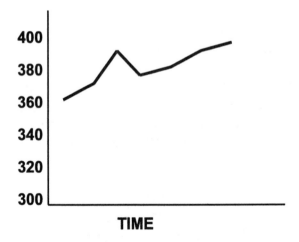

Step Three - Calculate the Moving Average

Now that you have charted the closing prices for the last seven days, you can calculate your first moving average figure. This is done by taking the seven closing prices and adding them together, then dividing by seven to give an average figure for the seventh day. If you add up your seven closing prices for Talking Widgets Plc, you get a figure of 2,671. Your average is therefore 2,671 ÷ 7 = 381.57. The value of 381.57 is now plotted on our chart on day seven.

To find the average for subsequent days, you simply take the total of the seven previous closing prices and divide by seven. The moving average figure for day eight would therefore by the sum of days two to eight divided by seven. Day nine would be the average of days three to nine, and so on.

When an average has been calculated for the seventh day onwards, a Moving Average line will have appeared on our chart, making it look something like this:

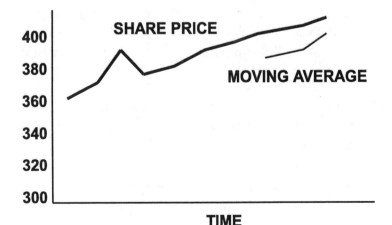

Now that you have a chart depicting the actual closing prices of Talking Widgets Plc and a seven day moving average line, you can begin to interpret their relationship. In brief, technical analysts believe that:

● If the share price line crosses the moving average line in an upward direction, a buy signal is generated.

● If the share price line crosses the moving average line in a downward direction, a sell signal is generated.

The Relative Strength Index

The Relative Strength Index - also known as the RSI - is a technical indicator which is believed to reveal whether a particular stock or market is overbought or oversold at any particular time. If a market is overbought then this may indicate there are too many investors holding shares. This suggests that a fall in market value will occur when some investors dump their stock in order to take profits. If a market is oversold then this may indicate there are too few investors holding shares. This suggests that more people will purchase shares and that the market will rise.

Mathematically speaking, the RSI is based on the ratio between previous price increases over previous price decreases, and can be expressed as follows:

$$RSI = 100 - \left(\frac{100}{\Sigma \; (+ \; changes \; / \; - \; changes) + 1} \right)$$

For those of you who find these types of formulas a little perplexing, this is how it is calculated, step by step...

The data you need to calculate the RSI is the *change* in closing prices of the stock or index you are dealing with. For example purposes you can use the same closing prices for Talking Widgets as you used a few minutes ago to create a seven day Relative Strength Index. Your data therefore reads something like this:

Day 1	360	+05
Day 2	370	+10
Day 3	394	+24
Day 4	380	-14
Day 5	385	+05
Day 6	387	+02
Day 7	395	+08

Now you should add together the sum total of the positive changes. These are the figures which are prefixed with an addition (+) sign. Your calculation is therefore:

$$5 + 10 + 24 + 5 + 2 + 8 = 54$$

In the same way, you now add together the sum total of the negative changes. These are the figures which are prefixed by a subtraction (-) sign. In your seven day sample there was just one negative change, so this automatically becomes your total.

$$14 = 14$$

This next step is to divide the total of positive changes by the total of negative changes, and then add one. Your calculation is therefore:

$$54 \div 14 = 3.85$$
$$3.85 + 1 = 4.85$$

Now you should divide 100 by the figure we have just obtained. Your calculation here would be:

$$100 \div 4.85 = 20.6$$

Finally, you take 100 and subtract the figure you just arrived at. This gives:

$$100 - 20.6 = 79.4$$

The Relative Strength Index figure for the seventh day is therefore 79.4. To calculate the RSI for subsequent days you simply carry out the same exercise on the data for the preceding seven days, in much the same way as you do when calculating a moving average.

Generally speaking, technical analysts work to the following principles:

● If the RSI is above 70 then the market is thought to be overbought and a fall in share price can be expected.

● If the RSI is below 30 then the market is thought to be oversold and a rise in share price can be expected.

The Moving Average Convergence / Divergence

Often abbreviated as the MACD, the Moving Average Convergence / Divergence technical indicator was developed by a man called Gerald Appel. It is a widely used oscillator created from the divergence between two separate moving averages - one calculated for the short term and another for the longer term.

When the underlying market is trending in one direction or the other, the shorter term moving average will rise or decline more rapidly than the longer term. The difference between the two averages is calculated and plotted on a graph as the oscillator line. As this line dips or rises above a control "zero line" so it is thought that the market may decline or rise respectively. The further the MACD oscillator moves from the zero line, the stronger the trend is thought to be.

The Price Momentum

This is defined as the ratio between the current market price of a commodity and the price of the same commodity x days ago. The formula for calculating price momentum is very simple:

$$(\text{Current value - value x days ago}) \times 100$$

If the momentum readings are high then this implies that the commodity is overbought and that a fall may be expected. If the momentum readings are low then this implies that the commodity is oversold and that a rise may be expected.

The Stochastic Indicator

This was developed by George Lane and is intended to measure - as a percentage - the position of a closing price in relation to the trading range of a previous time sample.

Stochastics are thought be useful because they work on the premise that the closing price of a commodity is usually closer to the top of the trading range during a rising trend, but closer to the bottom of the trading range during a declining trend.

By oscillating between a range of 0 and 100, the stochastic is thought to indicate the way the trend is moving. A stochastic reading at or below 30 might suggest that a market rise is due, whilst a reading at or above 70 might suggest a market fall.

Volume Accumulation Indicator

This technical indicator was created by Marc Chaikin. It measures trading volume in relation to price fluctuations, working on the hypothesis that if a market spends most of the day on a downward trend, but ends on a positive note, the positive trend should be interpreted in relation to the whole, which was largely negative.

The Volume Accumulation Formula looks like this:

Volume Accumulation = $(((MC-ML)-(MH-MC))/(MH-ML)) \times V$

Where **MC** is the Market Close, **ML** is the Market Low, **MH** is the Market High and **V** is the Volume.

This indicator is interpreted by comparing it with the market price and the appearance of prominent convergence's and divergence's are said to indicate likely changes in the market trend.

Putting Analysis to Work

If you want to start using technical analysis yourself then the best way of doing this is to begin by using both the Moving Average and the Relative Strength Index together.

By doing this you can use the RSI to confirm or reject Moving Average signals, and professional analysts believe that this improves the overall forecasting accuracy of both. The working guidelines which many successful investors use are as follows:

- If the moving average indicates that the share price or market will rise, and the relative strength index is below a value of 70, a rise in market value has been confirmed. The lower the RSI value is, the more confident you can be.

- If the moving average indicates that the share price or market will fall, and the relative strength index is above a value of 30, a fall has been confirmed. The higher the RSI value is, the more confident you can be.

- If the moving average indicates that the share price or market will rise, and the relative strength index is above a value of 70, ignore the signal. The RSI and the moving average are giving opposing advice.

- If the moving average indicates that the share price or market will fall, and the relative strength index is below a value of 30, ignore the signal. Again, the RSI and the moving average are giving opposing advice.

A Word of Caution

Whilst technical analysis is used widely throughout the investment world, it is by no means infallible. The fact is that technical analysis, as powerful and all-knowing as it can sometimes appear, is based only on past performance. It cannot take into account budget announcements or other human factors which will affect the markets, and so has no way of predicting "shock" crashes or booms. It should therefore be obvious that unless you are prepared to suffer losses when following incorrect buy or sell signals, professional advice should always be taken.

Summary

✔ Technical analysis is the art of predicting whether a financial market or share price will rise or decline according to the interpretation of historical data presented in the form of a **chart**.

✔ The **Moving Average** is the most popular technical indicator in use, and it is one which is employed by small-time private investors and professional corporate investors alike.

✔ The **Relative Strength Index** - also known as the RSI - is a technical indicator which is believed to reveal whether a particular stock or market is overbought or oversold at any particular time.

•✔ Technical Analysis, useful as it is, cannot take into account budget announcements or other **human factors** which will affect the markets, and so has no way of predicting "shock" crashes or booms.

Chapter Ten

Equity Options

KEY FEATURE: Equity Options are financial products in their own right which can be used to insure the investor against falling share prices or, alternatively, to generate profits from share price fluctuations without buying the shares themselves.

TO PUT it very simply, an equity option is something which gives the investor the right - but not the obligation - to buy or sell shares at a predetermined price. There are two types of equity options, and these are:

- **Call Options** which give the investor the right to *buy* shares at a known price.

- **Put Options** which give the investor the right to *sell* shares at a known price.

Before discussing how Calls and Puts can be used by investors, there are a few fundamentals which first need to be covered...

To begin with, equity options are bought in units of one contract, and a contract gives the investor control over a certain number of shares (usually 1,000) for a limited period. The price paid for an option contract is known as

---

the **exercise price** and the date on which the contract expires is known as the **expiry date**.

The exercise price of an option depends on a number of factors, such as how long the option has to go before it expires and where the exercise price is in relation to the underlying share price. These factors are known as **time value** and **intrinsic value**.

Time Value

Obviously, the longer you have an option to buy or sell shares, the more time there is for you to generate a profit. A share has more chance of increasing or falling substantially in three months than it has in just one. Therefore, the more time value there is in an option, the higher the exercise prices for that option will be.

Intrinsic Value

This is based on the relationship between the exercise price of the option and the underlying share price. If you buy a call option which gives you the right to buy 1,000 Ocepoc shares at 550p each, and the actual share price is currently 600p, then you have 50p of *positive* intrinsic value. On the other hand, if the current share price was only 500p then you would have - 50p of *negative* intrinsic value. A third possibility is that the share price is currently 550p, giving you zero intrinsic value.

● An option which has positive intrinsic value is said to be **in the money**.

● An option which has negative intrinsic value is said to be **out of the money**.

● An option which has no intrinsic value is said to be **at the money**.

What moves option prices?

Option prices move according to the type of contract and the movement of the underlying share price. If the underlying share price goes down then a call option (which gives the right to buy shares) will also go down, but a put option (which gives the right to sell shares) will go up. On the other hand, if the underlying share price goes up then a call option will go up, but a put option will go down.

For example, if Ocepoc shares are currently 600p each, the prices might be as follows:

Option		Calls			Puts		
		Jan	*Apr*	*Jun*	*Jan*	*Apr*	*Jun*
Ocepoc	*550*	50	70	80	12	20	25
(600)	*600*	30	50	60	30	40	45
	650	15	30	50	55	60	65

If you wanted to secure the option to **buy** 1,000 Ocepoc shares at 600p each until June, you would pay £600 for a Call option (60p x 1,000 shares per contract = £600). If the Ocepoc shares rose in the meantime, the option you hold would increase in value. On the other hand, if the actual share price fell, the value of your option contract would also fall.

If you wanted to secure the option to **sell** 1,000 Ocepoc shares at 600p until June, you would pay £450 for a Put option (45p x 1,000 shares per contract = £450). If the Ocepoc shares fell then your option would increase in value. On the other hand, if the actual share price rose, the value of your contract would fall.

Equity options are commonly used in one of two ways. The first is to help the investor insure against falling share prices and the second is to try and generate profits from share movements without buying the shares themselves. The best way of explaining these uses is to provide examples.

Options as Insurance

Imagine that you have shares in Ocepoc plc and you want to insure against a fall in share prices. To accomplish this you could purchase a put option so that if the share falls in value, your put option increases in value. If the share rises in value then your put option would fall in value, but you can then sell this option and continue enjoying the rising shares.

By adopting this approach, what you lose on one part of the investment you gain on the other. Of course, the number of options you use will depend on the size of your share-holding, but you can see from this simple example that whether prices go up or down, your losses are minimal, if not eliminated altogether.

Options as Investments

More speculative-minded investors use options to benefit from share prices without bothering to buy the underlying shares. For example, if an investor believes that Ocepoc shares are going to rocket in value, he can simply buy a call option at a fraction of the cost of the shares themselves. If he is right then the call option will increase in value and he can sell it at a profit. If he is wrong and the share prices fall then he can either sell his option at a loss or allow it to expire worthless.

If an investor believes that the shares of a particular company are going to plummet, he can benefit from this by buying a put option. If the shares do fall in value then his option increases in value and can be sold for a profit. If the investor is wrong and the shares rise in value, he can sell his option at a loss or allow it to expire worthless.

Although using equity options as speculative investment tools is too risky for many people, it does have a number of benefits:

● An option is almost always cheaper than the shares themselves. Just £500 can often give the investor the *right* to buy or sell 1,000 shares, but would seldom enable him to buy the shares. This gives the investor a lot of **leverage**, which means that he can make his money control more equity than if he bought the shares themselves.

● Options give the investor a specified risk. He knows at the outset how much he could lose in a worse case scenario if his option expires worthless.

● Potential gains are unlimited. If an investor holds a call option and the shares rise dramatically, his option will increase in value dramatically. If an investor holds a put option and the shares plummet, his option will allow him to generate great profits whilst everyone else is losing money hand over fist. It is not unknown for a successful options trader to enjoy profits which are literally thousands of times larger than his outlay.

The subject of equity options is vast to say the least. To attempt to discuss them in great detail in a book such as this would not do the subject the justice it deserves, so if you would like to study them further I highly recommend two other books in this series, **Understand Derivatives in a Day** and **Understand Financial Risk in a Day**.

This chapter should, however, have given you a glimpse into what many consider to be one of the most exciting - and useful - developments in the stock market for many decades.

Summary

✔   Equity Options are financial products in their own right which can be used to **insure** the investor against falling share prices or, alternatively, to generate **profits** from share price fluctuations without buying the shares themselves.

✔   A **Call** option gives the investor the *right* to **buy** shares at a known price.

✔   A **Put** option gives the investor the *right* to **sell** shares at a known price.

Conclusion

S O THERE you have it - a whistle-stop tour of the world of share investment. As I said at the beginning of this book, my aim has been to explain in simple terms exactly what shares are, how they work in relation to the stock market and how anyone can begin profiting from them as safely as possible.

You should now have enough knowledge to make an informed decision as to whether or not shares can help you to achieve your investment goals. If you think they can then the next step is for you to start studying the subject in more detail. If you have decided that shares are not for you, then at least this book will have saved you a lot of time and trouble.

For me, the stock market is like nothing else on earth. In my opinion, it is more than a casino where bets are placed. It is a microcosm of the world economy which gives us all the opportunity to invest in the companies which make a difference and help to build the shape of the future.

I hope that in this book you have come to understand that the world of shares is not as complicated as many people think. As you have seen, even professional forecasting techniques such as technical analysis can be adopted by the private investor. If this knowledge helps you to achieve professional profits then so much the better.

Best wishes,

Glossary

Bear
Someone who is of the opinion that the stock market will fall.

Bear Market
An underlying downward stock market trend.

Bearer Shares
These belong to the person who holds the share certificate. No register of shareholders is kept as far as bearer shares are concerned.

Bid
The price at which shares are sold.

Broker
A person who buys and sells shares on behalf of his clients.

Bull
Someone who is of the opinion that the stock market will rise.

Bull Market
An underlying upward stock market trend.

Capital Gain
The profit realised on an investment or asset when it is sold.

Capital Loss
A loss realised on an investment or asset when it is sold.

Convertible Preference Shares
These can be converted to ordinary shares on specific dates at predetermined rates.

Cum-Dividend
A security or share which allows the investor to receive all of the interest which has accrued since the last official dividend payment date.

Cumulative Preference Shares
These are Preference Shares which give the share-holder the ability to claim any unpaid dividends at a later date.

Deferred Shares
These do not normally qualify for dividends until a

predetermined date or profit level has been reached.

Dividend
A share of profits paid to a share-holder.

Equity Options
Financial products which give the investor the right - but not the obligation - to buy or sell shares at a predetermined price.

Ex-Dividend
A security or share which does not allow the investor to receive any interest which is due on the next official dividend payment date.

Exercise Price
The price paid for an option contract.

Expiry Date
The date on which an option contract expires.

Inflation
A reduction in the purchasing power of money due to a sustained increase in the Retail Price Index.

NAV
The Net Asset Value of a company.

Offer
The price at which shares are bought.

Option
See Equity Option.

Ordinary Share
The most common type of shares in the modern market, giving the share-holder the right to vote at share-holder meetings.

P/E Ratio
The Price Earnings Ratio of a company.

Penny Share
A Penny Share has a low price in relation to the broader market.

Preference Shares
These give the share-holder preference over ordinary share-holders in the list of payments to creditors.

Redeemable Preference Shares

These are more like loans than true shares, because they have fixed repayment dates.

Share

A share in the financial future of a company.

Shareholder

A person who owns one or more shares.

Spread

The difference between the Bid and the Offer, also known as the Bid-Offer Spread.

Technical Analysis

The art of predicting whether a financial market or share price will rise or decline according to the interpretation of historical data presented in the form of a chart.

Tax Loopholes for the Ordinary Taxpayer   **£4.99**

This book could save you a fortune. You don't have to be rich to take advantage of tax loopholes which could save you hundreds and even thousands of pounds. By Stefan Bernstein.

Understand Bonds & Gilts in a Day   **£6.95**

This handy title shows potential investors, and those with an interest in the bond markets, how to assess the potential risks and rewards, giving a simple to follow set of criteria on which to base investment decisions. Having shown the inexperienced investor how to go about buying bonds, it also teaches even the most arithmetically shy how to calculate the yield on a bond and plan an income based portfolio. The confusing terminology used in the bond market is clearly explained with working definitions of many terms and a comprehensive glossary.

Tax Self-Assessment Made Easy   £5.99

The book tells you what you have to do and when to do it, warning you of what happens if you don't. Chapters include:

- Self-employed and the effects
- Record keeping requirements
- People on PAYE
- Directors and trustees
- Penalties and surcharges
- What companies need to do.

A valuable glossary and a variety of concise appendices make this book the complete and essential guide with schedules to help you ensure that your tax bill is correct in the first place.

The Complete Beginner's Guide to The Internet   £4.95

Everywhere you turn these days, it's Internet this, Cyberspace that and Superhighway the other. Indeed, hardly a day goes by without us being bombarded with information and reasons why you should be on the Net. But none of that is of much help in making an informed decision about joining and using the Internet.

What exactly is The Internet? Where did it come from and where is it going? And, more importantly, how can everybody take their place in this new community?

The Complete Beginner's Guide to The Internet answers all of those questions and more. On top of being an indispensable guide to the basics of Cyberspace, it is the lowest priced introduction on the market by a long way at a *surfer-friendly £4.95* (alternative books cost around £30).

Complete Beginner's Guide to Windows 95   £4.95

- ❑ If you've just bought a new PC it will almost certainly be running Windows 95. You may need a helping hand to get started, and this book will serve as your introduction to Windows 95.
- ❑ If you've decided to take the step up to Windows 95 this book will be a steadying hand to the new and to the different.
- ❑ If your office, school or college requires you to use a Windows 95 computer, this book will quickly show you the basics so you can get on with your work.
- ❑ Even if you're already using Windows 95 but simply want to do more with it, this book will teach you some neat tricks.

The Complete Beginner's Guide to Windows 95 is a low-cost, easy to understand guide, specially designed for everyone who hates wading through hundreds of pages of information to find a simple answer.

Understand Derivatives in a Day   £6.95

By understanding how derivatives affect apparently safe investments, such as pensions, endowment mortgages and equity plans,
you can make sure your own cash is in good hands.

Nick Leeson and Co.'s dealings in the derivatives market ruined a
well-respected bank. How could this possibly happen? How could a
teenager run up a several hundred thousand pound debt by trading in
options? And, perhaps more importantly, how do derivative traders
earn their huge bonuses?

Learn...❑How private investors get started... ❑To Hedge, Straddle and
control Risk... ❑Ways to limit the downside but *not* the upside...
❑About *risk free* derivative strategies... ❑Trading Psychology - Fear,
Hope and Greed...   ❑Also, the History of Derivatives; Currency
Speculation; Long and Short puts; Tarantula Trading; and much more.

Understand Financial Risk in a Day   £6.95

Risk management is all about minimising risks and maximising
opportunities. Those who understand what they should be doing,
as a result of their risk calculations, will usually come out as
winners. Those who flail around in the dark will, more often
than not, be the losers.

Understand Financial Risk in a Day is a perfect introduction to the
subject. Light on detailed formulae and heavy on easy-to-follow
examples it will lead the reader to a greater awareness of how to
evaluate the risks they are facing and adapt a strategy to create the
best possible outcome. All of the latest risk management techniques
are discussed and the best tools selected for dealing with each aspect.

ORDER FORM

Please return to: TTL, P.O.Box 200, Harrogate, HG1 2YR.
Please rush me copies of : _____

_____

_____

❑ I enclose a cheque/payment for £_____ made payable to 'TTL'
❑ Please debit my Access/Visa card number   Signature:
☐☐☐☐☐☐☐☐☐☐☐☐☐☐☐☐☐   Expiry date: ☐☐☐☐

Name: _____

Address: _____

_____

_____ Postcode: _____

Please allow 14-21 days delivery. We hope to make you further exciting offers in the future. If you do not wish to
receive these, please write to us at the above address.   shares